All art work is owned by Jeanmarie Frost.
All rights reserved. No part of this book may
be reproduced, scanned,or distributed in any
printed or electronic form without
permission.

Dedication

I dedicate this book to my grandsons:
Jonny, Seni, David Christopher
David William, Nathaniel, Landen
& all future grandchildren.

Acknowledgments

All my love to all my children:
Jerusha, Anna, Danielle, David, & Patricia
A special thank you to Jerusha for giving
me the idea for this book and for Patricia's
continued encouragement to finish.
A thank you in loving memory of my sister
Peggy for giving me the love of art
starting at age 4.

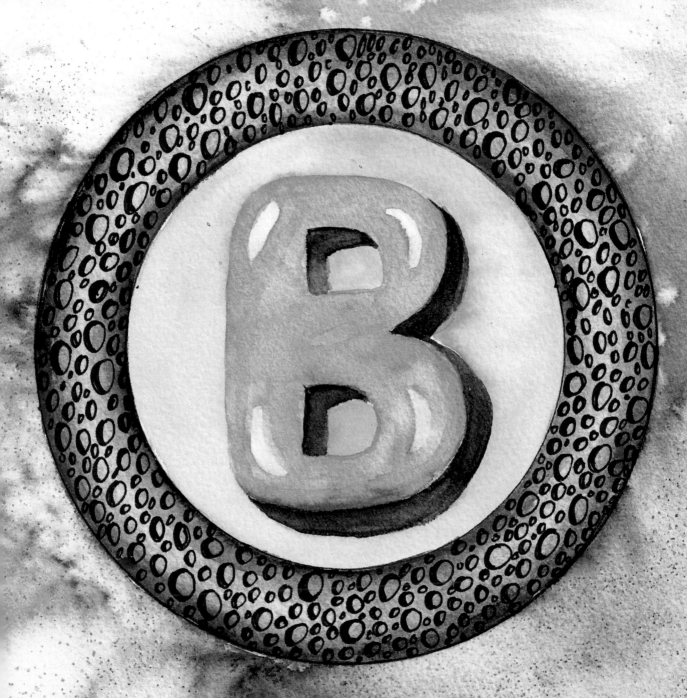

BELIEVE

CARING

DREAM

ENERGY

INSPIRE

LOVE

MEDITATE

NAMASTE

QUEST

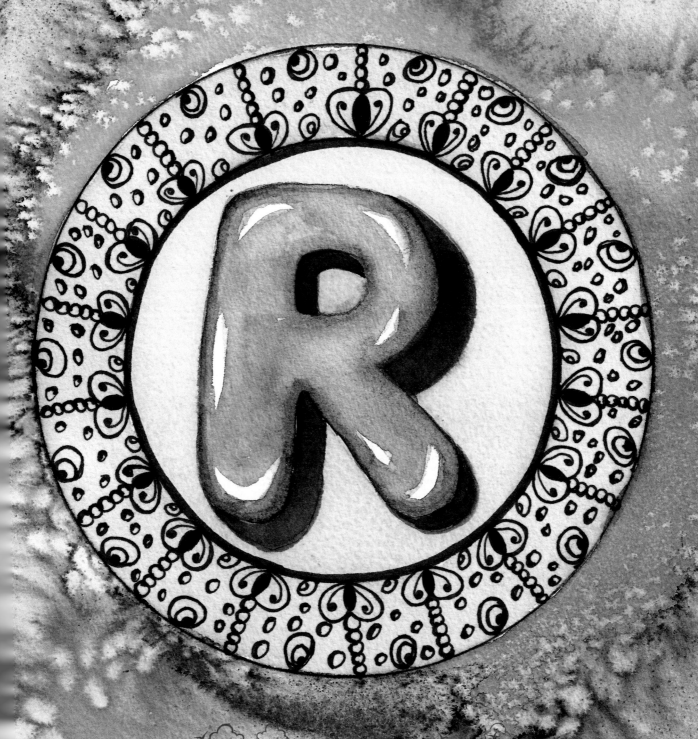

REIKI

SHANTI

TRUST

UNITY

VISION

WHOLENESS

ZEAL

ALPHABET meanings

ANGEL – messenger of God

BELIEVE – accept something as true

CARING – displaying kindness and concern for others

DREAM – a cherished ideal

ENERGY – life, spirit, spark, power, zip,

FAITH – trust, confidence, belief in God, Creator, Source

GENTLE – kind, considerate, sweet tempered

HAPPY – joyful, merry, smiling, lighthearted, radiant

INSPIRE – encourage, excite, influence

JOY – happiness, delight

KIND – thoughtful, unselfish, helpful, friendly, generous

LOVE – fondness, tenderness, warmth, caring, kindness

MEDITATE – focus in silence to be close to Creator/

NAMASTE • a greeting: "The Spirit within me honors the Spirit in you"

OM • Sanskrit word for supreme entity, God, Creator, Source

PEACEFUL • calm, relaxing, soothing, restful

QUEST • in search of something , looking for something, journey,

REIKI • a type of healing which channels energy from healer to patient

SHANTI • peace

TRUST • faith, confidence, to believe

UNITY • harmony, agreement, oneness, wholeness

VISION • daydream, hope, insight into the future

WHOLENESS • unbroken, undamaged state of being

XOXO • hugs and kisses

YIN/YANG • symbol for complementary opposites, such as dark/light, night/day, feminine/masculine, moon/sun.

ZEAL • great energy, excitement, enthusiasm

Jeanmarie (Merrill) Frost: Author and Artist

Jeanmarie is a mother of five children:
4 daughters, 1 son, & a Nanna of 5 grandsons
plus 1 adopted grandson.
Art is her passion as well as her family.
She strives to spread love and joy to family,
friends, and to the Universe.
Favorite saying:
"Love is the answer."

Made in United States
North Haven, CT
08 March 2022

16919146R00020